Once Upon a Life:

Stories for my Grandchildren

ELAINE MARIE (SIMEONE) PACE

Once Upon a Life: Stories for my Grandchildren

Elaine Marie Pace

Published by 1st World Publishing
P.O. Box 2211, Fairfield, Iowa 52556
tel: 641-209-5000 • fax: 866-440-5234
web: www.1stworldpublishing.com

First Edition

LCCN: 2017917797

Softcover ISBN: 978-1-4218-3798-7

This book is dedicated to my grandchildren:

Cora Marie Barclay

Gannon Robert Pace

Andrew Pace Barclay

Julie Grace Prickitt

Nathaniel Dominic Barclay

With thanks to the family members, living and deceased, who told me these stories.

INTRODUCTION

Many people wonder about the history of their families. Often someone in the family creates a family tree to show the birthdates and names of family members from many generations. That information is interesting but, in my opinion, it tells little about who the ancestors really were. I think, instead, that people's stories tell the most about them. Where did they come from? How did they grow up? What did they do when they were faced with problems or special challenges? Did they believe in a God? Could they overcome adversity? (Adversity means when bad things happen to you.)

As you grow up, your parents will tell you many stories about how they grew up and the values that they believe in. They will probably tell you, too, many stories about us, your grandparents. But I created this book to tell you stories about the people in your family who lived long before you. You never met those people but you are related to them. If they hadn't lived, you would not be living today. Their stories, like yours, are important.

In the old days when extended families lived near each other, they often would get together for dinner. When I was your age, my father's family and my mother's family gathered every Sunday afternoon and on every holiday to have dinner and talk. That's the way much of the family history was passed on. But our extended family doesn't live near one another so we miss those opportunities. That is why I want to share these stories now. I write them as a conversation. Pretend we are sitting at my house on a Sunday afternoon as the stories unfold. Your grandpa Dude and I have lots to tell!

Grammy
September 2017

Once upon a time every person was a baby with a mother and a father, grandparents and great grandparents, and sometimes brothers and sisters. The people who lived before us are called our ancestors. People who come from the same ancestors are called a family. Each family has a name like Pace or Prickitt or Barclay. On the next page I have drawn a picture of your family tree. I will tell you some stories of what life was like for the people in our family tree. Most of these stories came from conversation with our parents, aunts and uncles, and grandparents.

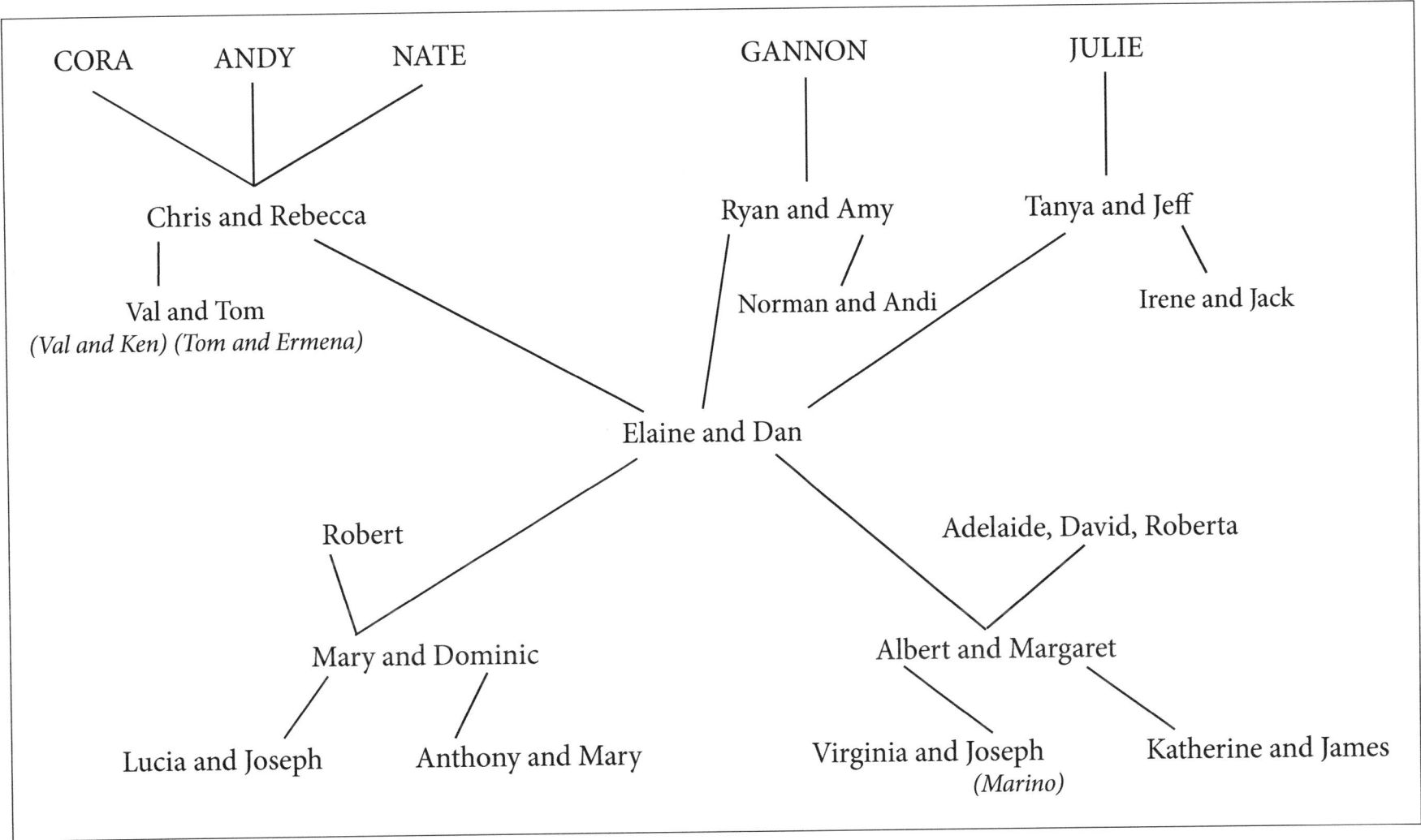

FAMILY TREE

CORA   ANDY   NATE

GANNON   JULIE

Chris and Rebecca

Ryan and Amy   Tanya and Jeff

Val and Tom
(Val and Ken) (Tom and Ermena)

Norman and Andi

Irene and Jack

Elaine and Dan

Robert

Adelaide, David, Roberta

Mary and Dominic

Albert and Margaret

Lucia and Joseph   Anthony and Mary

Virginia and Joseph
(Marino)

Katherine and James

Once upon a time people didn't have Smartphones with cameras in them. To get a picture of the family, people called a photographer who came to the house with a great big camera and took a picture of the family. Here are some pictures of our parents and grandparents taken nearly one hundred years ago. Their stories may surprise you.

The first picture is a baby shot of Margaret Gannon, Dude's mother. Her father James Gannon is holding her. Her mother Katherine (Dewire) Gannon is holding her younger sister Adelaide. The picture was taken in Donora, Pennsylvania.

Next is a picture of Dude's mother Margaret Gannon when she was a young girl. She is sitting in the middle of the picture. She was born in Donora, Pennsylvania on April 22, 1910. On the left is her sister Adelaide and on the right side are her brothers Vincent and James. James did not live to grow up. He died at ten years old. He had a disease called rheumatic fever that hurt his heart. Another brother named William was born into this Gannon family in 1917. Poor little William died a year later in 1918. He died during a terrible flu epidemic in our country, the United States. We are lucky today that we can get a flu shot each year so that few children today die of the flu. No one had invented a flu shot then.

The Gannon family came from Ireland on the continent of Europe. We live on the continent of North America across the Atlantic Ocean from Europe. If people wanted to come from Europe to America, they traveled on passenger ships across the ocean. The trip took a long time. Sometimes the ships took two weeks to travel from Europe to America. No one in our families traveled by airplane in those days.

Life was hard in Ireland. Many of the people there grew potatoes on their farms in the countryside. Potatoes were the main food for the people of Ireland. Suddenly in the 1800's the potatoes got diseased and died. That time was called "the potato famine". When the potatoes died, people did not have enough to eat. Many starved and died. Life was very hard.

Margaret's father's ancestors came from the town of Roscommon in the county of Connaught in the north central part of Ireland. Roscommon was located between Dublin on the east coast and Galway on the west coast of Ireland. Roscommon was a market town where many people traded agricultural products and livestock in those days. Livestock are animals like cows and goats and pigs. The Gannon family ancestors worked for a Duke who owned a large farm. Because of the potato famine, the Gannon family moved from Roscommon to Lancaster in England. James, Margaret's grandfather, was born in Lancaster, England.

When he was 17 years old, grandfather James took a boat from Liverpool, England, to America. He made his way to Scranton, Pennsylvania. He worked as a helper in a puddling furnace of the Lankawanna Iron Company and later the Carnegie

Steel Company. Puddling furnaces are very hot ovens that help to make iron or steel. He married a woman named Mary Smith. James left Pennsylvania and took his family to Minnesota where they lived and worked on a wheat farm during 1881 and 1882. But the family missed Pennsylvania and moved back to Pittsburgh. James got his old job back at Carnegie Steel. He had a son who also was named James.

In Pittsburgh, young James met a girl he liked a lot. Her name was Katherine Dewire. James and Katherine got married and they moved from Pittsburgh to 106 Castner Avenue in Donora, Pennsylvania where Margaret was born and grew up. Margaret's father James worked as an accountant in a steel mill.

Katherine was born in Kittanning, Pennsylvania. Katherine's parents also emigrated from Ireland. Emigrated means that they left to come to America to build a better life. Katherine's mother's name was Hester Dempsey. She was born in Ireland where she married Daniel Dewire. Together they made the long, arduous boat ride. Arduous means very difficult. Hester hated the boat ride. The Atlantic Ocean waves were very bumpy and the boat rocked and reeled. Hester said a prayer that, if she and Daniel arrived safely in America, she would never go back to Ireland. She and Daniel settled near Pittsburgh, Pennsylvania, where they lived for the rest of their lives as their family grew. Their daughter Katherine had a daughter named Margaret, Dude's mother. Margaret gave birth to a son named Daniel. Here is a picture of Katherine Gannon holding her grandson Daniel, your grandfather who you all call Dude.

My family name was Simeone, and my father's name was Dominic. To the left is a picture of Dominic with his father Anthony, his mother Mary Pasciuto Simeone, and his sisters and brothers. Dominic was the oldest in his family. His brother Vincent is on the top left. Dominic stands on the top right. His sister Teena stands in the middle, and his brothers Eddie and Al are sitting at the bottom of the picture. Do you see any differences between the way children dressed in those days and how you children dress in 2017?

These children grew up as all children do. Below is the Simeone family when they were older. In the middle the father and the mother are sitting. My father Dominic is standing behind his father on the back right.

One Simeone family member is missing from this picture. In 1920 Dominic lost a sibling named Annie. She was a victim of the terrible flu epidemic of that time. Annie was three years old when she died, and Dominic was four. He had spoken very clearly but after she died he started to stutter. It was hard for him to pronounce many words no matter how hard he tried. My father told me that, when he was in high school, he felt terrible when the teacher called on him to speak in class. Dominic stuttered his whole life. Today there are many ways that doctors and nurses can help children who stutter but no one knew what to do to cure stutterers in those days. To the left is a picture of Dominic with his sister Annie.

The Simeone family came from a seaside town called Gaeta in Italy but Anthony, the father, and Mary, the mother, brought their family to America. Dominic was born on March 30, 1916 in Massachusetts where his father Anthony settled. Anthony had a fruit market in Somerville. As they grew older each of his sons helped him work in the fruit market. Every morning the family got up at 4:30 to feed their horse. Then Anthony, my grandfather, rode the horse from Somerville to Boston to buy fruit to sell in his market that day. The fruit market was located in Teele Square, Somerville, Massachusetts. There were no trains or subways or buses then. Before my grandfather had a car, he got around on a horse.

Anthony was frugal. That means he saved his money carefully. The Simeone family moved from an apartment on 100 Washington Street, Somerville, to a house on 37 Prescott Street, West Medford, Massachusetts. After Anthony bought a house for his family, he saved more money and bought more houses, fixed them up with the help of his sons, and sold or rented them. He was a successful businessman.

Many years later when my parents Mary and Dominic were married and moved to Massachusetts, Anthony built an apartment for them behind his house on Prescott Street. The address was 39 Prescott Street and that's where I lived when I was five to ten years old.

The Simeone family was proud to be Italian. Dominic's family spoke only Italian in his home. When Dominic went to school, his parents said, "Dom, your job now is to learn English and teach the rest of the family how to speak the English language properly." He did. Dominic was a good student and worked hard. He had a paper route in the neighborhood and delivered newspapers to many houses. The newspapers cost two cents each in those days.

Dom put the money he earned into a bank account and saved $432. That was a lot of money at that time. Four hundred thirty-two dollars is the same as more than a million dollars today. But something terrible happened in 1932. It was called The Great Depression. President Franklin Roosevelt had to close all the banks and everyone lost their money. Dominic was sad but he didn't give up. He started saving all over again. That happened to a lot of people during the 1930's, so many new laws were passed when the Depression was over to help protect people from losing their savings the way Dominic did.

People who lived through The Great Depression learned to be very careful with everything they owned. They didn't waste anything. Dude's parents, Margaret and Al, did not have tissues or paper napkins in their house because they didn't want to make waste or throw things away. They used cloth napkins and handkerchiefs instead. To save space in the trash, Margaret rinsed out cans from soups and vegetables, put them on the kitchen floor, and stomped them until they were crushed.

When he attended Medford High School in the early 1930's, Dominic studied two foreign languages: Latin and French. He chose to study those languages because he wanted to go to Harvard University nearby in Cambridge, Massachusetts and Harvard required its applicants to learn two new languages other than English. Harvard invited Dominic to go to that college, but his father needed him during the daytime to help run the fruit market or repair the houses he bought. Dominic went to Bentley College at night instead. He obeyed his father. That was called "duty". He gave up what he wanted because his father needed him to do something else to help his family.

Dominic's parents could not afford to send five children to college so each one saved enough money to pay for their own schooling. Immigrants who came to America from other countries worked hard to be educated and to get good jobs in America. Many immigrants still do that today. Here is a picture of Dominic when he graduated from Medford High School.

Many Americans think it is their duty to protect their country, and they join the military. In the United States of America the biggest military teams are the Army or Navy or Air Force or Coast Guard. When Dom was about twenty-three years old, a terrible war broke out in the world. It was called World War II. A mean dictator named Adolf Hitler was doing terrible things to many German people (who did not have blond hair and blue eyes). These people were Jews. Hitler ordered that a sign be placed above the doors on the homes of Jewish people so that the German army could capture them and take them away. These mean German army people were called Nazis. The United States and England and France and Russia got together and decided as a team to fight the Germans to make Hitler stop his

mean behavior. The United States fought in the war for four years and their side finally won. Dominic and his brothers joined the Army and went off to fight in that war.

About a year before he left to do his service in the Army, Dom met Mary DeFederico from Connecticut. She was the daughter of another immigrant Italian family. She had a cousin who lived near Dominic's family in Massachusetts. Once when she visited her cousin she met Dom and they fell in love and got married. Here is a picture of them taken on their wedding day, April 10, 1944. You can see that my father is wearing his Army uniform. I still have that uniform in my closet.

Dominic's mother put a flag in her front window for each of her boys who were off fighting in World War II. The Simeone boys returned safe and sound. Many other families weren't so lucky. They lost brothers and husbands and fathers in that war. Here is a picture of me with my mother and my cousin Janice. Janice never met her real father because he was killed overseas in World War II.

While Dominic served as a staff sergeant in the Army, Mary moved to Connecticut to live with her mother. Dominic and Mary's first child Elaine Marie was born on June 14, 1945 at Bristol Hospital in Bristol, Connecticut. Dominic was far away when his first child was born. The Army sent him to work in North Africa. He worked as an accountant. He was lucky that he didn't have to shoot guns in the war. The soldiers on his team sent a telegram from North Africa to Connecticut to congratulate Mary. In those

days, people sent messages by mail or telegram. Letters came across the Atlantic Ocean from Europe or Africa to America by boat. Sometimes it took two or three weeks or more for a letter to arrive. (No one called by phone in those days either. Few people had phones and those who did had to share the line with others. If you wanted to make a call and picked up the telephone and heard another voice using the line, you had to wait until the other person finished talking before you could make your call. Neither did we have computers or Internet in those days.) Here is a picture of my great grandmother holding me, her great granddaughter Elaine Marie, in front of my grandmother's house on a county highway in Bristol, Connecticut.

This woman, my great grandmother Carmela Tommaro, was one of my favorite older relatives when I was a child. She spoke only Italian so, until I was five years old and moved from Connecticut to Massachusetts, I spoke and understood Italian. In her bedroom on the second floor of my grandmother's house she created a small altar with a cross and votive candles and a kneeler like the kind you find in some churches. She lit her candles and prayed there every day.

When Carmela was young, she and her husband Camillo really wanted to have a baby. Though she tried, she could not become pregnant. She lived with her husband in a small farming village called Fondi, near Naples in Italy. The families who could not keep or take care of their newborn children gave them to the priest and he brought them to the village square for other families to choose as their son or daughter. My great grandmother and her husband decided to get a baby that way so they went to the village green to meet the priest on the designated day. Only one baby was there. An infant girl born in 1895. They chose her and named her Lucia. Lucia was my grandmother. Many years later, when she became an adult, Lucia returned to Italy to try to find out who were her real parents. She even tried to bribe the priest but he kept the secret of the baby who was born "on the wrong side of the blanket". That is an old expression the Italian people used when a baby was born before the parents got married.

When it was time for her to get married, Lucia's parents chose a husband for her. He was nineteen years older than Lucia. She did not get to choose a husband as most people in our country do today. An Italian man named Joseph DeFederico became her husband.

Joseph had gone to America to find work and build a better life. After he found a good job as a stationmaster on the New

York, New Haven, and Hartford Railroad, he wanted to marry and start a family. He wrote a letter to his parents and asked them to find a good wife for him. His parents were friends with Lucia's parents, Camillo and Carmela Tommaro. The parents all decided that Lucia would be a good wife for Joseph even though they had never met. The parents put Lucia on a boat and sent her to Newark, New Jersey, where the boat docked. Joseph met her and took her to his house (provided by the railroad) in Bristol, Connecticut. They married and had five children – four girls and one boy. (My mother Mary was one of those children.) Lucia invited her parents to live with her in America. In those days, families tried to live close together.

Joseph, my mother's father, died when he was still in his forties, so Lucia had to bring up their five children all alone. She spoke very little English. Her children got jobs as early as they could and gave their earnings to their mother to help with the living expenses of the family. My mother Mary was very bright and an excellent student. When she was in junior high school the principal promoted my mother two grades ahead instead of one because she was so smart. But Mary quit school at 16 and worked in the post office in Terryville, Connecticut. She felt it was her duty to help support her family.

When my grandmother Lucia was approximately sixty years old, she studied to become an American citizen. Everyone in the family was very proud of her. Here is a picture of Lucia and me on the day of my graduation from Regis College in 1967. Because she had such a difficult life, she was especially happy that all her grandchildren had the chance to go to college and get good jobs.

My family was called middle-class. We weren't rich but we weren't poor either. At the time when I graduated from college, most middle-class college girls became secretaries, teachers, or nurses. Most also married and started families when they were very young. I was twenty-three when I married Dude and twenty-seven when I had my first baby. Today most women and men wait until they are a bit older before marrying and starting families. On the next page is a picture of Dude and me on our wedding day, August 10, 1968. We were married at noon in Saint Brigid's Church in Lexington, Massachusetts.

While most of my family settled in Massachusetts and Connecticut, most of Dude's family settled in western Pennsylvania. He was born in Pittsburgh on May 1, 1945. His ancestors came from Ireland and Italy. Dude's grandfather's name was Joseph Pautasso. He was born in 1879 and came from Prato Botrile, a small Italian village in northern Italy. (If you google Prato Botrile you can watch some videos of the beautiful mountains and countryside there.) But Joseph Pautasso thought he could have a better life if he

came to America. He married a woman named Virginia Chiampo who came from the same town. They got on a boat and sailed across the Atlantic Ocean to America. They arrived in New York City in July 1904.

Joseph and Virginia traveled from New York to Scranton, Pennsylvania, where Virginia's brother was living. Then Joseph brought Virginia to a town in western Pennsylvania called California. He picked that town because he could get a job in a coal mine nearby. Joseph and Virginia had two boys named Joseph, Jr. and Albert. Albert was Dude's father. Albert was born in California, Pennsylvania, in the year 1906. Sadly, Joseph was killed in a mine accident. Albert and his brother lost their father. Virginia lost her husband. It was a sad time.

Joseph's salary had paid for all their expenses. Now Virginia had no money and no job. Most of the jobs in the community were in the coal mines and women didn't work in the mines. The Italian women in the town wanted to help Virginia. They gave her food and a room to live in. They helped to care for her little boys. One day a peddler named Marino Pace came to California. He was selling pots and pans. Virginia came out of the house where she was staying and looked at the pots and pans. "I like them but I am a widow with two young children," she told Marino. "I don't have any money to buy them."

Marino left the town of California to continue his peddling in the mining towns between California and Homer City, Pennsylvania. He was a widower himself. His wife had died. He kept thinking about Virginia and her two little boys and decided to return to California and ask her to marry him. She said yes and moved with him to Homer City. Marino became the new father to Albert and his brother Joseph. He adopted the boys as his sons. That's how our family got the name Pace.

Virginia and Marino later had a sister named Louise and another sister named Luigetta who was born in 1909, but Luigetta died in 1910. She was only one year old. She died of the flu. Medical care for children wasn't as good in those days as it is now. There were no pediatricians then. One doctor served many people of all ages. Doctors traveled from town to town on a horse. They treated sick people in their homes.

Now that Marino had a family he decided to stop peddling pots and pans. He opened a furniture store in Homer City. His family lived upstairs on the second floor of the store. A scary thing happened to his store on Thursday, April 22, 1915. The local newspaper, *The Indiana Weekly Messenger*, reported that at 12:03 a.m. someone lit twelve sticks of dynamite and blew up the first floor of his store. (The police figured out the time of the attack because Marino wound up all his clocks before going to bed at 11:00. The clocks on the first floor stopped at 12:03. The police thought that the jolt of the blast caused the clocks to stop.) All the furniture, crockery, and Queensware were shattered and lay in pieces all over the floor. (Queensware was a very beautiful type of Wedgewood pottery that was made in England in 1765. Many antique collectors still value Queensware today.) Luckily the upstairs floor was made of cement or the Pace family might have been badly injured. This was the third time in Homer City history that a dynamite prank was played. The police couldn't figure out who would do such a thing. Everyone liked Marino. He had no enemies.

Marino's name appeared in another newspaper, *The Indiana Evening Gazette*, in December of 1922 and March of 1923. Those years were a time called Prohibition. To prohibit means to stop something. The government decided that drinking liquor or alcohol was bad and they banned it. Prohibition became a law all over our country. Alcohol or liquor were often called "spirits" in those days. No one could buy spirits any more. But lots of people loved to drink alcohol so they learned how to make their own spirits in secret places like their cellars or garages. Some people made the liquor for themselves. Others sold it. That was called bootlegging. In December of 1922 Marino Pace's name appeared in the police column because he did some bootlegging. Nine other names were accused of bootlegging on that same day. Three months later, in March of 1923, Marino was called to court and fined $1000 for making and selling liquor. I guess he didn't learn his lesson the first time he was warned.

Dude's father Albert was a brave and hard-working man. He once worked for a company that built bridges and he climbed to the tippy top of bridges under construction. His mother Virginia was very nervous about that job. Once she even walked to the job site where he worked and shouted, "Get down off that bridge, Albert. You're going to kill yourself!" Albert saved the money he earned and he put himself through college to become a chemist. He spent his whole career working for the same company. The name of the company was Duquesne Light.

Margaret, Dude's mother, studied to be a teacher. To be a teacher in those days you attended two years of college. The colleges that trained teachers were called normal schools. Margaret graduated from normal school in California, Pennsylvania. She was licensed to teach English and geography. She once told me that she really enjoyed working with special needs students. Here is a picture of her during her teaching days.

When her first child Adelaide was born, Margaret stopped working and stayed home to raise her family. Many families, who could afford to do that, chose to have the mother stay at home rather than take a job outside of the home. Here is a picture of Dude's family on his sister Adelaide's wedding day. (Adelaide is the bride. Her mother and father stand beside her. Kneeling on the left is David Pace and on the right is Daniel, Dude. Standing between David and Dude is their little sister Roberta.) Dude still misses his brother David. David was killed when he fell off a bridge on his way to work in 1972. Every family faces some happiness and some sadness. This was a sad time for everyone in the Pace family but pictures like these remind them of happier days. Below is a picture of David with Margaret and Roberta at Ocean Grove, New Jersey, where they vacationed every summer.

Dude's father Albert and his mother Margaret had a long marriage that began with a bit of strife. Strife means trouble. Margaret's Irish mother Katherine didn't want her to marry an Italian man. Margaret and Albert went to the priest at their church and told him they loved each other very much and wanted to get married. The priest said, "Come to the 7:00 a.m. mass and I'll marry you afterward." He did. Margaret wore an ordinary brown dress and her mother never came to the wedding. Her sister Adelaide was her witness. They had no pictures of their wedding day.

A few years later, when her sister Adelaide married an English-Irish gentleman who was called Scotty because he lived in Scotland, everybody wore festive clothes. Here is a picture of Margaret

19

dressed up for her sister Adelaide's wedding. Dude's grandmother, Margaret's mother Katherine, later regretted her prejudice. She saw that Albert was a fine man who took good care of her daughter and his family. She apologized because she had tried to stop them from marrying. She realized that Italians were good people. Sometimes people are afraid of people they don't know very well.

Our mothers led very organized lives. Monday was always wash day. Clothes were washed in large sinks called set tubs until ringer washing machines became popular. A ringer washing machine is a large tub of water with a ringer on top. After the clothes were swished in warm soapy water in the tub, the mothers took each piece of wash and fed it through the ringer. Here is a picture of a ringer washing machine.

After using the ringer the mothers filled a laundry basket with the damp clothes, put a bag of clothespins on their shoulder, and hung each piece of clothing on a clothesline in the back yard. I have happy memories of following my mother into the yard to hand her the clothespins when I was very young. When I got taller, I enjoyed clipping the clothes to the line all by myself. I remember how excited my mother was when my father replaced her clotheslines that stretched between wooden poles and set up a clothesline with a pulley so that she could stand in one place and take the clothes off the line by using the pulley. No one had invented clothes dryers yet. When the clothes were dry, the mothers took them off the line and saved them in folded piles until Tuesday, ironing day. My mother ironed everything, even sheets and pillow cases.

My father, who was an accountant, and Dude's father, a chemist, were paid once every two weeks. Each man gave his paycheck to his wife. My mother and Dude's mother took care of all the household expenses with the earnings of their husbands. They cashed the paycheck and put money in several envelopes that they labeled to cover the bills. One envelope said "electricity", another said "gasoline", another said "mortgage". A mortgage is money you borrow from the bank to buy a house. You pay back the loan every month by sending money to the bank. After several years, you've paid enough money to own the house all by yourself and don't need to pay the bank any more.

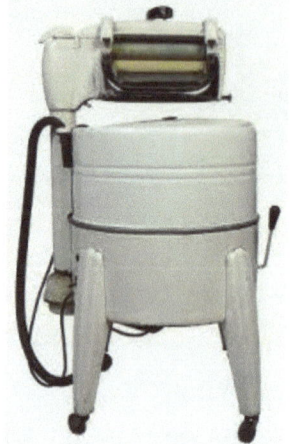

During the 1950's when I grew up, families were very proud to have a house and a car. We didn't know anyone who had more than one car in a family. Some families had no cars and had to take the bus or streetcar everywhere they needed to go. Here is a picture of Albert, on the left, with a car popular in the 1930's.

On Sunday afternoons, after we got home from church and ate our big dinner of the day at 1:00, my mother cleaned up the kitchen and my family (Mom, Dad, my brother Robbie, and me) piled into my father's 1947 bright yellow Ford sedan and took a drive. During the warm weather months, we stopped for ice cream. I remember once when my father didn't feel like going out for the Sunday drive and my mother cried. She needed that outing. She had been home working in the house all week. Dad gave in and we went.

Another envelope that the mothers filled when the paycheck came home was labeled "groceries". The mothers had to plan to have enough money to feed the family for two weeks. We ate little meat when I was young. We might have a pork chop dinner on a weekday or a roast beef meal on Sunday, but my mother made various pasta or vegetable meals during the rest of the week except on Saturday night. Every Saturday night we'd eat a Yankee meal – hot dogs, hamburgers, baked beans, and a salad. That was a tradition in the Boston area. Dude's mother served steak every Saturday night and lots of peas during the week. Dude hates peas to this day! His favorite meal was chipped ham, a thin ham stewed in barbecue sauce and served on a roll.

In those days a loaf of bread cost twelve cents, a dozen eggs cost twenty-five cents, and a quart of milk cost about thirty cents. Many of the stores where the mothers purchased items gave out S&H Green Stamps for every purchase. You'd get one green stamp for every ten cents you spent. The mothers pasted the stamps into little booklets and, when the booklet was full, you could trade the stamps for something you needed. Once my mother got a whole set of kitchen knives with the green stamp booklets she had filled.

Grocery stores also tried to attract shoppers by offering free products. My mother shopped at the grocery store once each week. (There was no such thing as Amazon Fresh that delivers groceries to your doorstep.) My mother walked to the market and pulled a grocery cart behind her. Each week, when she paid for her purchase, she got a free encyclopedia. An encyclopedia is a set of books that contains lots of information. You can look up a word like "airplane" and learn all about airplanes. You can look up a word like "dogs" and read everything you may want to know about dogs. That's how encyclopedias worked. Each book in a set of encyclopedias is called a volume. There were about 20 volumes in a set of encyclopedias. So it took twenty weeks for my mother to get the full set of encyclopedias. Most folks were proud to have a set of encyclopedias and placed them on shelves in their living rooms. (In those days living rooms were called "parlors".) Words like "space ship, computer, satellite, monorail, and technology" were missing from those encyclopedias. Those things hadn't been invented yet. Most people don't have sets of encyclopedias in their homes anymore because they use computers and information systems like Wikipedia to look things up and learn about them. We can ask Siri too.

The milkman delivered milk to the stoop outside our back door every week. The milk came in quart-sized glass bottles. The milk was pasteurized to get rid of germs but it wasn't homogenized. Homogenized means it's shaken up so that the milk and cream mix well. In our bottles of milk, the cream rose to the top of the bottle. If you wanted creamy milk, you shook the bottle. If you wanted fresh cream for your cereal or oatmeal, you scooped the rich cream off the top of the bottle.

When our parents were young, the price of a ticket to a movie was twenty cents. The mothers and fathers had to decide whether the family could afford to go to the movies or whether they needed to save the money from the paycheck for groceries and other necessities. It wasn't until I was much older that I realized the value of the five dollars my mother put in one envelope for my weekly piano lessons.

A very special event in the lives of Dude and me was when our little brother and sister were born. Dude was seven years old when his sister Roberta was born. Dude carries this picture of his little sister in his wallet to this day.

I was six years old when my baby brother Robbie was born. (Robbie's full name was Robert Anthony Joseph Simeone. The two middle names were the first names of our grandfathers.) My mother decided that, with a new baby, she didn't have time to take good care of my hair so she gave

me my first haircut. She was very sentimental and saved the hair. Before she died in 2010, she gave me that box of hair that now is more than sixty years old!!!

To the right is a picture of me helping to hold Robbie when he was two months old. It is the day of his baptism. He wears the same outfit that I used for my children on their days of baptism. Our granddaughter Julie wore that outfit on her baptism day. That outfit is 72 years old and has now served three different generations.

Our families went to the Catholic Church every Sunday and on special holy days during the year. Catholics are Christians. In the Catholic Church children are baptized when they are infants. When they are about seven years old, they receive their First Holy Communion. Here is a picture of me with my brother Robbie on his First Communion day. Notice that all the girls and women wore hats and white gloves to church and petticoats under their full skirts in those days. Very fashionable!

And here is a picture of Rob and me with our parents and our own families many years later.

Dude was an altar boy when he was eleven, twelve, and thirteen years old. He helped the priest to celebrate Mass at St. Bernard's Church, a short walk up the hill from his home on 1416 Grandin Avenue, Pittsburgh. He and his mother walked to church for the 6 a.m. Mass on many mornings. He helped the priest get ready for the service then stood on the altar with the priest during the Mass. Afterward he helped to rinse out the chalice that contained the wine used at communion time. He was a rascal. Sometimes, when the priest wasn't looking, he took a sip of the wine! On the next page is a picture of Dude with all the other altar boys at St. Bernard's Church. Girls weren't allowed to serve on the altar in those days. Can you find Dude in this picture?

The man on the left in the picture is the priest of the church. The teacher on the right is a nun. Her name was Sister Cornelia. A nun is a woman who joins a religious group called an order. Nuns live together and pray a lot. They also do good deeds like teaching school or helping in a hospital. Look at the nun's clothes. Her outfit is called a habit. Her habit is a long black tunic with a white cowl collar and scapular that frames her face. We children were always curious about what color hair the nuns had because their hair was covered. "Do they even have hair?" we'd ask. Some nuns don't dress in habits any more but, when Dude and I were young, all the nuns wore habits. From the belt on the habit hung a string of big beads. The beads were called rosary beads. The beads made a clicking sound when the nun walked. Many Catholics had small strings of rosary beads in those days. You'd sit in a quiet place, put the beads in your lap, and say prayers like the Our Father or Hail Mary as you moved your fingers along the string of beads. Each bead represented one prayer. A Catholic rosary had 59 beads. Other religions use prayer beads too. Saying the rosary is one way to meditate.

Our childhood years were very different from the lives of kids today. If a nearby school had a playground, it contained only a swing set, a slide, and maybe a see-saw. We had no inflatables or Chucky Cheeses or even McDonalds. Our mothers cooked most of the food we ate. We rarely went out to a restaurant although my family walked to church every Sunday morning and stopped at the local donut shop afterward. Each person in my family selected a donut, put it in a brown paper bag, and took it home to eat with coffee or milk. I was sure happy to get that donut because, in those days, we were not allowed to eat or drink anything before we had Communion at church every Sunday.

Another important weekend ritual was our Saturday night bath. Both Dude and I grew up in families that took one bath every week, on Saturday night, so we'd be all clean and fresh for church on Sunday. We had only one bathroom in our house and in it sat an old white claw-footed tub made from heavy cast iron. The tub was called "claw footed" because the feet holding the tub looked like giant claws. Our mothers put a few inches of warm water into the tub for our special bath time. We had no showers in those days.

We kids loved to go out and play after dinner in the summer months. Dude ran around in the woods near his home in Overbrook, a part of Pittsburgh, Pennsylvania. Many evenings my cousin Janice and I met friends on the Brooks School field across the street from our West Medford home and played hide and seek until our mothers shouted our names from their doorways as the sun began to set. In those days, our black friends lived on one side of the railroad tracks and our white friends lived on the other side, but the black boys and girls came over to that playground to play with us nearly every night all summer long. We had lots of fun!

A very exciting day in our childhoods was the day when our families got their first television set. We were seven years old. The TV set was a huge box with a screen on the front. The back of the box unscrewed. Inside were lots of different cathode ray tubes that helped the TV to run. When the TV conked out, our parents called the TV repair man. He'd come to our house, unscrew the back of the TV cabinet, and replace a tube or two to get the TV working again. Here's what the television sets of the 1950's looked like.

Sometimes the picture on the TV screen got very fuzzy. To help the picture to be clear, our parents bought a device called rabbit ears and placed it on top of the TV. By moving the rabbit ears in different directions you got better reception. The rabbit ears served as an antenna. We had no wi-fi in those days. Why do you think this device is called "rabbit ears"?

Our parents and grandparents did not have televisions in their homes when they were young but most homes had a radio. On Saturday afternoon my father and his brothers gathered around the radio and listened to sports events. They loved to hear the radio announcer describe the innings of the Red Sox baseball games. "One strike, one ball, two strikes, two balls, three balls, full count, out!" Dude's father listened to sports on the radio too, but he also loved to listen to the Texaco Opera Hour every Saturday afternoon. The broadcast came live from the Metropolitan Opera House in New York City.

Dude and I loved to read. When I was as young as seven years old, I'd walk all by myself over the railroad tracks near my home at 39 Prescott Street in West Medford on my way to the public library. Our libraries contained just books – no playrooms, toys, or computers. We loved reading stories about real people. By the time we were nine years old, Dude and I had read every one of our library's thirty orange-bound biography books about famous people like Daniel Boone, Davy Crockett, Benjamin Franklin, Clara Barton, and Amelia Earhart. Dude and I are happy that you grandchildren love to read too. Here's a picture of my father Dominic reading with Rebecca when we visited Williamsburg one Thanksgiving.

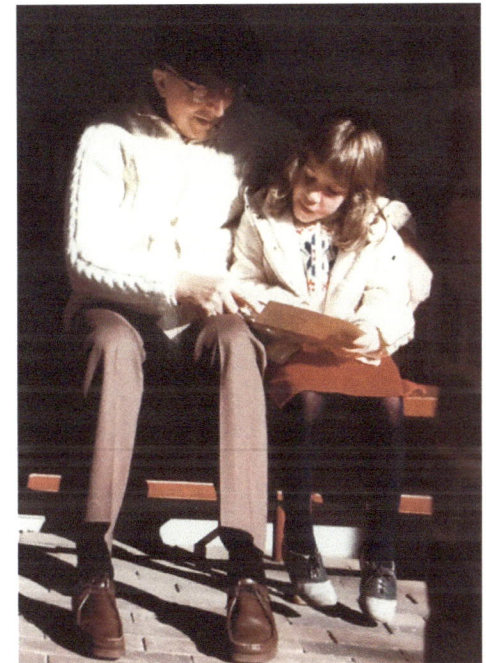

As we grew a little older, both Dude and I learned to play an instrument. I played the piano. All alone I'd walk from our West Medford house to the town square. My piano teacher lived on the second floor over a store. She was very nice, especially one day when I didn't feel well and threw up all over her piano in the middle of my lesson.

I started taking piano lessons when I was six years old after I quit dancing school. Even though I loved the cute tutus we got to wear for our dance recitals, I wasn't very good at dancing. I couldn't even do a cartwheel! My mother suggested that I try taking piano lessons instead.

Dude played the saxophone and, when he was in junior high and high school, he marched

in his school's marching band. When we were 21 years old and got to know each other, we were happy to find out how much each of us loved music. Just as Dad's father Albert loved opera music, my father Dominic loved Broadway musicals and taught me to love them too. During the 49 years of our marriage, Dude and I have enjoyed all kinds of music. Classical, opera, and Broadway musicals have been our favorites but we also love church music, rock and roll, jazz, country music, popular tunes, and even the rhythm of rap.

We didn't have as many opportunities to be on teams as you children do today but I enjoyed Brownies and Girl Scouts and Dude loved to play baseball in Little League. He was a good hitter and played third base when he was in the field. Dude was also a great swimmer and swam on his high school swim team. During the summertime, when he wanted to go to South Park, distant from his Overbrook home, he hitchhiked with his sister Adelaide, his brother David and other friends. They got into a lot of trouble for doing that. Their mother Margaret was furious with them for hitchhiking. She was also upset that they went into a public swimming pool when so many children were getting the disease called polio.

Polio stopped some children from breathing and made others wear braces on their legs. In 1955 when we were in fourth grade, Dr. Jonas Salk invented a vaccine to prevent kids from getting polio. He was a doctor from Pittsburgh. Dude's elementary school, St. Norbert's in Overbrook, was chosen to try out the first polio vaccine. He remembers how his classmates all went outside to the school playground in the springtime and, one by one, each was given a polio shot. Some people were upset because they worried that the shots would fail and the children would be hurt. Luckily, the vaccine was successful. I remember the day we lined up along the hallway outside the nurse's office at my school, the Brooks School in West Medford, to get the polio vaccine.

Because my mother was so afraid of polio, I wasn't allowed to swim in public pools when I was young and lived in the city. I had lots of fun jumping waves with my father at Hampton or Salisbury or Revere Beach where we went every summertime. When we moved to the town of Lexington from the city of West Medford, I was the only one of all my friends who didn't know how to swim. I'd sit on the edge of the pool at pool parties and pray that no one pushed me in. I finally took swim lessons at the YMCA in Pittsburgh after I was married. I've enjoyed swimming in pools, lakes, and in the ocean all the rest of my life.

Here is a picture of me in my bathing suit ready to swim. My mother and her sisters weren't allowed to wear bathing suits. My grandmother Lucia was very modest and old-

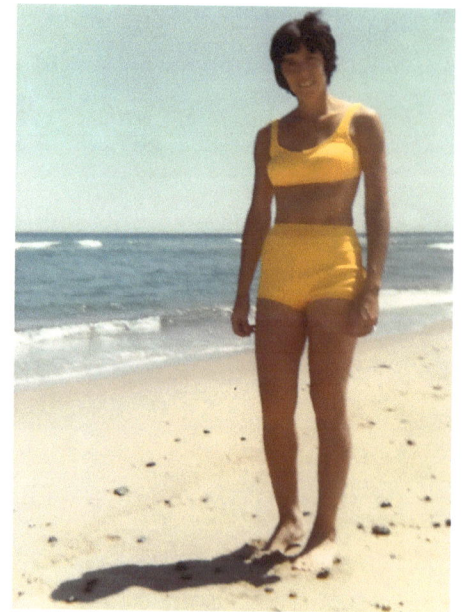

fashioned. She didn't think that girls should show their legs in public. My father bought my mother her first bathing suit in Savannah, Georgia, where they lived after they were married.

I loved to write when I was in high school, and I became the editor of my high school newspaper. That means that I read all the articles written for the newspaper, picked the good ones, and helped to figure out how they'd be arranged on each page of the newspaper. The teacher who helped us with the newspaper is still my friend today. We exchange Christmas cards every year. Her name is Rebecca.

Dude and I had jobs when we were very young. Dude delivered newspapers. Sunday was his favorite delivery day. He'd pile the heavy newspapers in his red wagon, sit on top, and race his cart against the cart of his friends down the steep hills of Dormont. The heavy papers made the cart go super fast. My family had a red wagon too. The wagon was called a Radio Flyer.

When my grandfather Anthony wasn't working at his store in Somerville, he grew a big garden at his home in West Medford. He owned more than one acre of land that stretched to Alewife Brook. He also raised chickens. It was exciting to go into the chicken coop and gather the eggs from the nests. I had to hold the eggs very gently so they wouldn't crack. Sometimes the eggs were warm.

Anthony planted lots of tomatoes and corn and lettuce and beans and carrots, beets, and other vegetables. My grandfather made wine out of the Concord grapes that grew on vines on the arbors over the pathway that led to the garden. He had a wine cellar and big casks where my father and his brothers helped make the wine. Children weren't allowed to go there.

My grandfather grew a crop of sweet raspberries that I loved to pick with my small fingers when I was six and seven years old. Picking raspberries is hard because they are very delicate. If you squeeze too hard, the raspberry squirts its juice and the berry isn't so nice any more. I would kneel near the bushes and pick for a long time to fill fifteen pint-sized baskets with the bright red raspberries. Then I'd put them into the Radio Flyer and walk down Prescott Street and around the corner. "Would you like to buy a basket of raspberries?" I'd ask after I rang the doorbell of each house. I got to keep all the money I earned. I was excited to have my own little business at such a young age. And I was very lucky too. On one of my first stops I came to a house where several elderly people lived. The woman who ran the house and took care of the people bought every single pint of my raspberries. The next year I went directly to that house with my raspberries. I worked very hard at the picking but I didn't have to work too hard at the selling.

I loved school. Every August my mother and I took the bus and then the train to downtown Boston from Medford Square to shop for new school shoes and clothes. Buster Brown saddle shoes were very popular in those days. In the shoe department of the store was an x-ray machine that looked like a tall bathroom scale. I'd step up onto the machine and a picture of the bones of my foot would be taken. That picture would help the shoe salesman to pick the correct shoes for me. Then we'd head to Filene's Basement where lots of clothes were sold at cheap prices. My mother and I would pick out a new blouse and a plaid skirt or maybe a new dress for me to wear during the next school year. Girls didn't wear pants to school in those days. The best part of the back-to-school shopping day was lunch at a delicatessen on Washington Street where I'd always order a Reuben sandwich and a chocolate milkshake.

Here's a picture of me on my first day of kindergarten. Kindergarten lasted only a half day in those days, and we had to take a nap in the middle of the morning. Bummer!

When I was in eighth grade I learned to sew my own skirts and dresses. I sewed my white linen college graduation dress and many cute outfits for my children when they were young.

Dude attended kindergarten at Overbrook Elementary School. His brother David walked him to and from school every day. When the kindergarten year ended, Dude transferred to St. Norbert's Elementary School where David also was a student.

Here's a picture of Dude and David when they were younger. They loved to play at the train station in Donora. They climbed onto the old wooden hand truck that the stationmaster used to haul heavy boxes into and out of the trains. I enjoyed playing on the wooden hand truck at my grandfather's train station in Bristol too.

In fourth grade Dude's parents bought a house on 4815 Grandin Avenue in Dormont and he then transferred to St. Bernard's School. Later, his parents sent him to South Catholic High School, a private Catholic high school run by a team of teachers called the Christian Brothers. The brothers were very strict but they were good teachers and Dude learned a lot. If you didn't obey all the rules, some of the brothers hit you. And if you were very naughty, those brothers said, "Get out. We don't want you here." If that happened your parents had to find another school for you. Dude was obedient. He studied, did all

his homework, and worked hard. He got to stay at that school all through high school. Here is a picture of Dude in 1963 when he graduated from South Catholic High School in Pittsburgh, Pennsylvania.

The first day of school was an important time for Dude and me when we became parents. We took a back-to-school first day photo every year. Here is a picture of your parents about to leave for their schools in Kinnelon, New Jersey, where we lived when they grew up.

My parents bought a new house after I finished the fourth grade. We moved from West Medford to 3 Essex Street, Lexington, Massachusetts. I wanted to go to Catholic high school because one of my friends was going to Matignon High School in Cambridge and another was going to a Catholic academy in Arlington, but my father said, "Lexington has one of the best school systems in the country and you're going to school right here." He was right. I met many kids from families different from mine and that helped me to grow in many ways in the years to follow.

Dude and his mother went back-to-school shopping at Gimbel's Basement in Pittsburgh. He hated those shopping days but loved the hot dog and ice cream cone at the end of the shopping trip. Here's a class picture of Dude's class in eighth grade at St. Bernard's Catholic School in Mount Lebanon. Count the number of children in his class. Do you have that many children in your class? Can you find Dude?

A happy memory of the start of school each year was getting a new pencil case -- a small box or zipped purse that contained a lead pencil, an eraser, and a pencil sharpener. Sometimes a little ruler was included in that case. The school gave us all our other school supplies. Here is a picture of Dude's St. Patrick's Day project made with his school supplies during his kindergarten year at Overbrook Elementary School. Can you figure out which school supplies he needed to complete this project?

As we moved into the upper grades at our schools, we got a book for each major subject: English, Social Studies, Science, and Math. The teacher gave us our books on the first day of school. We carried them home and cut book covers out of brown paper bags then fasten the covers to the books with Scotch tape. On the second day of school the teacher checked to be sure our books were properly covered. At the end of the school year, we'd return the books for other students to use.

When we were in high school, our parents made us get jobs. We couldn't be in many afterschool clubs or sports because we had to work. Dude found a job cleaning a thrift store. Later he worked hauling and delivering furniture for a company called Bevilaqua Brothers. That was very hard work.

During my junior high and high school years, I babysat, worked at a dry cleaner store, worked at a catalog order office of a store called Sears Roebuck, and even worked for a short while in the meat department of a grocery store called A&P.

Sears Roebuck was a very famous company because it was one of the first companies in the world to invite people to order clothing, tools, and lots of other things from a catalog. The first Sears catalog was published in 1888. The Sears catalog was very heavy. It had many thin pages with pictures and prices of all the goods you could buy. You'd go to the catalog order office where I worked or call Sears to order something. Sears even sold do-it-yourself house building kits. You could buy a kit and build your own house. Sometimes the items you ordered would take a few weeks to arrive. (That's certainly very different from priority ordering at Amazon today. Today we can order something in the morning and receive it in the afternoon!) We had no charge cards in those days. You had to pay cash or write a check for your purchases.

During the summertime when I was not in college, my Uncle Eddie got me a job in an office at Digital Equipment Corporation, a Massachusetts company that made computers. Dude came to that company from Pittsburgh to learn how to program a computer, and that's how we met. On the next page is a copy of the letter I got saying I was hired to work during the summer I met Dude.

digital equipment corp

MAYNARD, MASS. 01754
TWinoaks 7-8822 TWX MAYN 816

May 3, 1966

A happy summer... I meet Dan!

Miss Elaine M. Simeone
3 Essex Street
Lexington, Massachusetts

Dear Elaine:

A review of our 1966 summer work requirements has been completed.

As a result of your interest in summer employment with DEC we are pleased to offer you a summer position in our Training Department under the supervision of Mr. Robert Pate at the rate of $1.85 per hour.

DEC's policy concerning summer employment cannot allow any free time away from your working period with us this summer. The reason for this is that you will be acting as a replacement for many of our employees who will be taking their scheduled vacation during the summer months.

Please contact us as soon as possible if you are interested in this position and give us a date on which you will be available to work.

I will look forward to hearing from you shortly.

Sincerely,

Joseph F. Gaffney
Personnel Assistant

JFG/mmb

An office secretary typed letters like this one by using a machine called a typewriter. The typewriter had a keyboard like the keyboards on your computers and IPads today. Unlike our computers though, the typewriter had a roller. You would take a piece of paper and roll it into position so that the metal keys hit the paper and printed one letter at a time onto the paper each time you hit a key on the keyboard. You had to type carefully because the typewriter had no delete key. If you made a mistake, you'd have to insert a little piece of paper with white chalk in front of the mistake. You'd type the mistaken letter again and the white chalk would make the mistake disappear. Then you'd have to retype the correct letter over the chalk mark. The little piece of chalked paper was called "correctype". Typing was very tedious compared to the way we do word processing today. On the next page is a picture of a typewriter used during the 1960's.

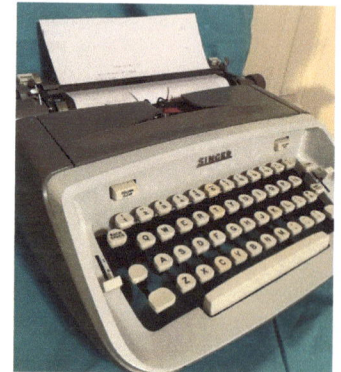

When he was in college Dude's favorite subject was English but his father said, "I will not pay for your college costs if you major in English." Albert thought that Dude could get a better job if he learned math and science, so Dude studied math and science instead of English. He commuted on a streetcar to the University of Pittsburgh. To commute means to travel to and from college every day. After college, Dude studied at Georgetown University in Washington, D.C. He learned how drugs are made and how medicines act when they are given to people. He then became what is called a "pharmacologist". He worked in New Jersey for a big drug company named Hoffmann LaRoche. The company came to America from Basle, Switzerland. Dude traveled to Basle and all over the world doing work for that company.

I went to an all girl's Catholic college called Regis College in Weston, Massachusetts. I lived there with many other girls in a big building called a dormitory. A dormitory contains many small bedrooms where the students sleep at night. I shared my room with one roommate named Patricia. She lives in Seattle today. We are still good friends.

In 1967 and 1968 after I graduated from Regis I attended Johns Hopkins University in Baltimore, Maryland. I learned how to be an English teacher. I taught eighth grade students in Towson, Maryland. Then I taught tenth graders in Penn Hills, a town outside of Pittsburgh. I looked very young and sometimes kids mistook me for one of the high school kids. Once, when I sat on a bench in the school office waiting to talk with the principal, a large girl who always got into trouble for saying bad words leaned over and whispered to me, "Hey, what'd you do?" She thought I was in trouble too. At that school in Penn Hills teachers paddled naughty students. But I never paddled anyone.

The year of 1968, when I graduated from Johns Hopkins and started teaching in Penn Hills, was a tumultuous time for our country. Tumultuous means crazy and very confusing. Many people were prejudiced. That means that some white people did not like black people and treated them unfairly. Many black people did not trust white folks either. Even today in 2017 some people are still prejudiced against people who aren't like them. When Dr. Martin Luther King, a peaceful black leader, was shot by a white man in the springtime of 1968, riots broke out all over our country. Black people were furious. White people were afraid. Crowds of angry protesters gathered and did violent things. They threw bottles into the windows of stores. They stopped traffic. They started fires. I remember going to the rooftop of my apartment building in Baltimore, Maryland, and seeing the fires burning all over the city. Our country's leaders had to call out soldiers with tanks and guns to quell the crowds in cities all over the country. Quell means to calm them down. Sometimes the angry protesters even clashed with the soldiers. This fighting went on for many weeks. When it finally stopped, people remained angry and afraid.

In 1968 when I taught in Penn Hills, an armed soldier was stationed outside my tenth-grade classroom. Soldiers were sent into schools to help to keep violence away. Penn Hills had been a town of mostly white people for years and years. Homewood, a part of Pittsburgh, was the town next to Penn Hills. In Homewood many black people lived. The year that I started teaching tenth grade at the brand new John Linton Intermediate School in Penn Hills, the school was integrated for the first time. Buses

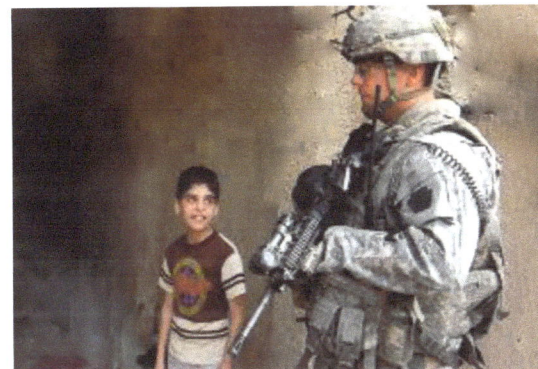

brought black kids from Homewood to school in Penn Hills. The white people were afraid. The black people were afraid. They didn't know each other and some didn't cooperate very well. They bullied and even fought on the playgrounds at recess time. Finally the National Guard was called in to help keep order. The soldier outside my classroom was a member of the National Guard. I have many happy memories of that year of teaching but remember well how I closed my classroom door to shut out the image of that armed soldier outside.

I loved teaching. When I wasn't teaching in a school, I enjoyed teaching my own children, your parents: Ryan, Tanya, and Rebecca. Then, when they grew older, I resumed my career in education. I taught in elementary schools, middle schools, and high schools. My favorite job was elementary school principal in Parsippany, New Jersey. It was fun to see all the children learning and growing and to watch the good teachers teach. I became a superintendent of schools later in my career. A superintendent is the boss of all the principals. A principal is the boss of the teachers. And a teacher is a boss of the students.

Dude and I enjoyed our jobs but our families were very important to us. When I was young the Simeone family

celebrated all together twice each year and no one missed those gatherings. On the previous page is a picture of the Simeone side of the family at one of our gatherings. We were listening to our cousin Claire tell stories of her volunteer work in a country called Sudan in Africa. Can you find your parents in this picture?

Here's another family shot of both the Simeone and DeFederico families nearly 20 years later at the wedding of my brother's daughter Bethany. Your parents are older in this picture. Can you find them?

Dude had many cousins too. His Aunt Adelaide Lynch had eleven children. Dude remembers the fun he had playing with his cousins at his house in Dormont or at their home in Donora, Pennsylvania. Dude and I had 34 cousins in all! When they grew up, some of those cousins got married and had children and their children later married and had children. That's how a family grows.

At least once each year our family drove to Pittsburgh to visit our relatives and get together with some of the cousins. Margaret loved to see her family all together. We'd go to outings at places like South Park or Kennywood. Kennywood was an amusement park. Here is a picture of Margaret who went with us to Kennywood on one of those summer outings.

Every family has its good times and bad times. A bad time happened to Dude and me when we were married for only four years. We decided to get our first pet, a little kitten named Portia. When we got her, she was so small that she fit into my shoe. Dude and I had lots of fun playing with her.

In early April in the year 1972 we drove with Portia from Washington D.C., where we lived at the time, to Lexington, Massachusetts, to visit my parents for the Easter holiday weekend. As we were driving through the state of New Jersey on our way back to Washington on a road named the Garden State Parkway, another car hit our little blue Volkswagon bug. (The car was called a bug because it was very small.) That little blue bug had ferried us on camping trips across the country all the way to California and south through the Smoky Mountains. It was a very hard-working and faithful car a lot like the little engine that could. Our car was destroyed in the accident. No one ever found Portia. We had to stay in the hospital for a month. Everyone was worried about us. My mother was especially worried because I was pregnant. I was expecting my first baby. But five months later in Sibley Hospital in Washington, D.C. on a sunny September 26, 1972, I gave birth to a healthy baby boy. We named him Ryan David Pace. Dude was so happy.

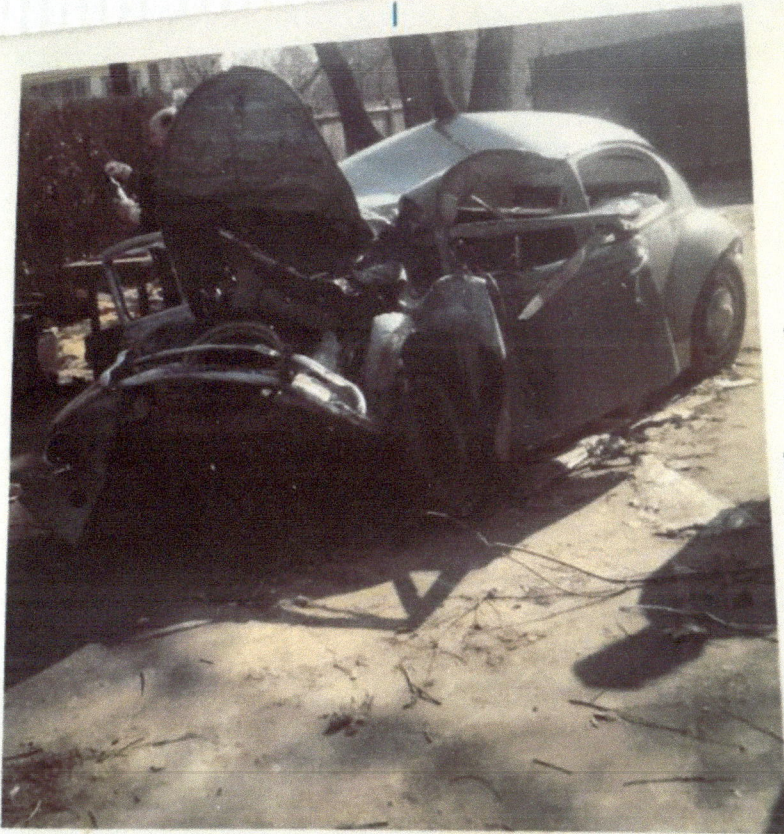

April 4, 1972

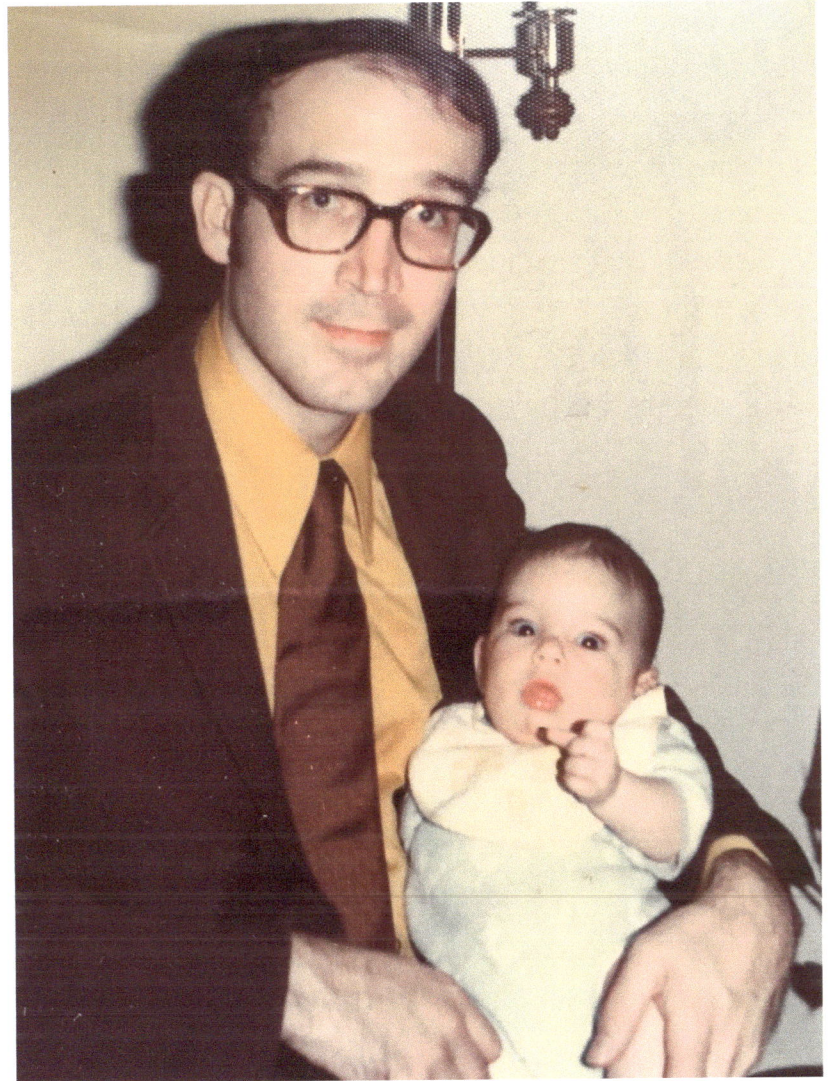

On October 25, 1974, in the very same room at Sibley Hospital where Ryan was born, Dude, Ryan, and I welcomed our first baby girl, Tanya Kristen.

Ryan was happy to have a sister. They played well together. He was a little bossy like many older brothers and sisters are, but she didn't mind. Until she was three or four years old she did every single thing he told her to do. But, as she grew a bit older, she became quite a tattle-tale. I got so tired of hearing her tell tales on her brother that I finally took a paper towel roll and called it a tattle tube. "You can only tattle through this tube," I told her. She'd come up to me, ask me to bend down, and put the tube against my ear while she whispered her tattle-tales.

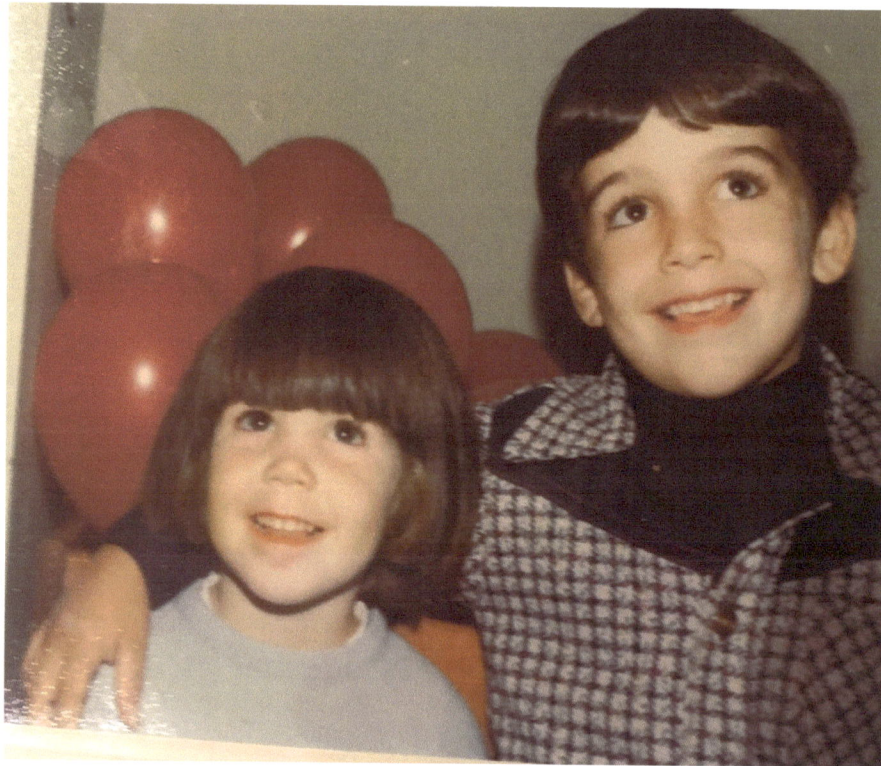

Our family of four became a family of five on October 28, 1978 when our second little girl, Rebecca Dawn, was born. We gave her the middle name Dawn because we were driving past the reservoirs in Kinnelon at dawn in the morning to get to Riverside Hospital in Boonton, New Jersey, the town where Rebecca was born. She waited a long time to come to us. We expected her two weeks earlier. Each day we waited and waited but she didn't come. Mary and Dominic, my parents, waited with us too. On the next page is a picture of Tanya welcoming her new baby sister at last.

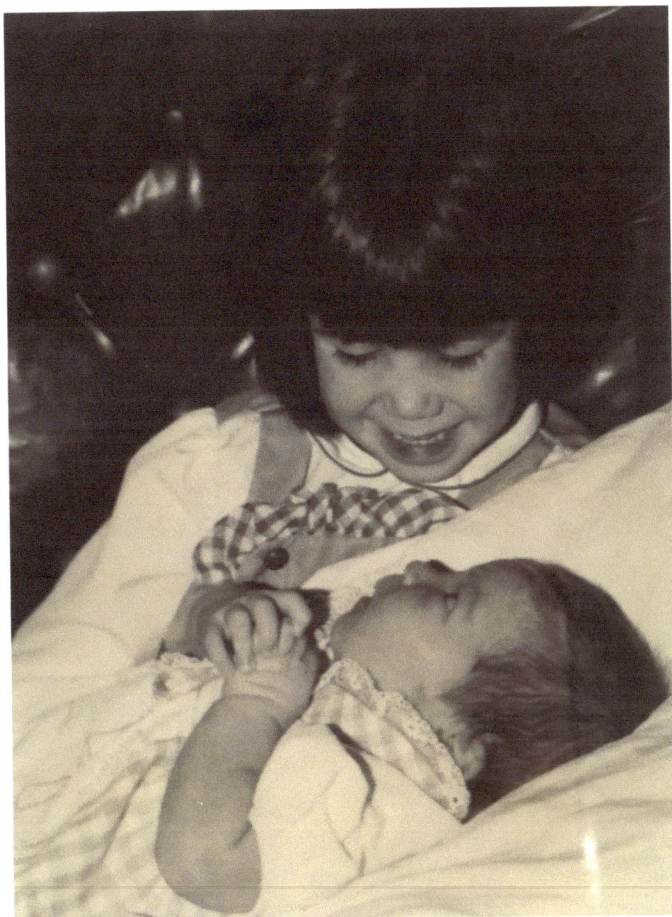

Our family included some pets too. We had three dogs: Britt, Tory, and Zachary. Britt was a Brittany Spaniel, Tory was a Sheltie, and Zachary is a cockapoo, a combination of a poodle and a cocker-spaniel.

You all know our energetic dog Zachary. Sometimes he's a pain in the neck but we love him and he loves us. He follows us wherever we go. He sleeps in our bed. We take him for walks every day. He's usually on a leash, but he loves to run free when we hike at Sepiessa Reservation or around the horse field trails near our house. You remember those fields, don't you? That's where you feed carrots to the horses every summertime when you come to visit us on Martha's Vineyard.

Zachary loves to run free along the ocean and jump into the salt water too.

Here we are having fun at Cedar Tree Neck Sanctuary in West Tisbury.

Our family had a few other pets too. Tanya had a goldfish named Happy. Rebecca had a kitten named Smoky.

On a June day in 1982 Ryan came home from school and asked if we could take care of his class gerbils for the summer. There were four gerbils. I agreed. Long before the summer was over the gerbils multiplied to twenty-four! Sometimes they got out of their cage and ran all over our basement and greenhouse. Dude couldn't sleep at night because he was worried that the gerbils would get stuck between the studs and the dry wall in the basement and die there and rot. Once when the cleaning lady came she found a dead gerbil on the brick floor of the greenhouse. "I didn't know whether to pray over it or sweep it up," she confessed. I was certainly happy to deliver that gerbil crew back to the school in September. We never had another opportunity to take care of class pets, thank goodness!

Every Sunday Dude and I brought our family to a Catholic church in Pompton Lakes, New Jersey. The church was named St. Mary's. We met many good people at that church. Each of our children received the sacrament of First Communion and was confirmed at St. Mary's Church. Here is a picture of Tanya's first communion day. Family members and friends would always join us for these special occasions.

Our family of five joined other family members when they had special occasions too. Here is a picture of our family in Pittsburgh all dressed up to celebrate Ben Mikita's baptism. Ben is the son of Dude's sister, Roberta.

When a baby is baptized in the Catholic Church, the parents choose a godmother and a godfather for the child. The godparent helps the child grow up to be a kind and good Christian person. My godmother was my Auntie Anne, one of my mother's sisters. She always made me feel loved. She was a sweet person inside and outside. That means that she looked pretty but she was kind and behaved well too. When she was young, the people of her hometown, Bristol, Connecticut, voted her the prettiest girl in town and she got to ride on a float in the city parade waving and smiling at everyone.

When we moved from Connecticut to Massachusetts in 1950, I started receiving packages from someone called my "secret pal". These packages would arrive on my birthday and on other special days like Valentine's Day. At Christmas time I'd always get an extra gift from my secret pal. "Who is my pal?" I'd ask my mother. With a twinkle in her eye, she'd say, "I don't know." She really did know but she kept it a secret. It was fun to try to figure out who that secret pal was. One day when I was nine years old a package from my secret pal arrived. I was smart enough to look at the postmark on the package. I saw that the package was mailed to me from Bristol, Connecticut. The mystery was solved. Auntie Anne was my secret pal.

Every summer for many years of my childhood I spent a week with Auntie Anne during my summer vacation. My parents drove me in their yellow Ford sedan on Highway 1 from Massachusetts to Connecticut, then they returned to pick me up

and bring me home on the next weekend. It was a long, slow ride in those days. We had no super highways like we do today. The drive took four hours each way. (Today it takes half that long.) I always got carsick. During the week when I visited, Auntie Anne took a vacation day from her job and we rode on the train from Bristol to Hartford where we went to a store called G. Fox. She bought me something pretty to wear, took me out to lunch, and then we boarded the train to return to Bristol. That week in Connecticut made me feel very independent and happy when I was a little girl of six, seven, eight, nine, and ten years old.

When we were children, Dude and I didn't go on many vacations because our parents didn't choose to spend their money on big vacation trips. If we went anywhere, we drove. (Neither Dude nor I ever traveled on a plane until we were twenty-one years old.) My family went on "day trips" during my father's vacation every July. A day trip is when you go somewhere and come back home on the same day. Our summer vacation day trips always included an outing to an amusement park and another to the beach. An outing is when you go out somewhere beyond your home town. Once we drove to the White Mountains in New Hampshire and hiked at Franconia Notch. We rented a small cabin and stayed overnight that time because the White Mountains were far from home and we couldn't get back on the same day. I remember that we stopped at a Chinese restaurant on the way home. My little brother exclaimed, "I hate Chinese food. I want a hamburger." The restaurant didn't serve hamburgers so he didn't eat much that day. He was very grumpy.

For one week every summer, Dude's family rented a house in a New Jersey town with a Methodist campground. The town was named Ocean Grove. Methodist folks are Christian. In those days Methodist people thought that it was good to have the same kind of people live close together, so they built small cottages in a place called a campground. No one except Methodists could build or buy houses there then. People who went to the Methodist Church were strict about honoring God on Sundays. No cars were allowed into Ocean Grove on any Sunday during the year. The rules for living in these campgrounds have changed today. Anyone can buy a house in the campgrounds. People other than Methodists can live there. We have a Methodist campground in the town of Oak Bluffs on Martha's Vineyard. Those campgrounds were built in the late 1800's and many of the houses are very cute, like gingerbread houses.

When your parents were children, we saved our money so that we could spend a week in the town of Eastham on Cape Cod in the state of Massachusetts. I picked that town because it was the headquarters of the Cape Cod National Seashore, an area from Eastham to Provincetown that was protected by our government so that the sandy beaches and dunes and grasses and kettle ponds would be preserved. Sometimes our leaders pass laws to protect beautiful places so that humans don't build them up too much and ruin them. That is called conservation. Because of conservation your parents, you, and your children will be able to enjoy the Cape Cod National Seashore for many generations.

We rented a house in Eastham and went to the beach every single day during that vacation week. We even brought all our bikes to Cape Cod so that our family could ride on the bike paths there. Dude worked for hours putting the roof rack on our Ford Country Squire station wagon. Then he attached all five bikes. Those bikes stood tall on the car's roof as we barreled down the highways from New Jersey to Massachusetts. I cooked our dinner every night except one. I used the cans and boxes of food that we hauled from our New Jersey home. On our last vacation evening, we went to a restaurant for dinner and ordered fish because the fish caught on Cape Cod was fresh and delicious.

Kinnelon, New Jersey, was the town where Dude and I raised our family. We lived in one house on Woodland Court and another on Highlands Drive. Kinnelon was a pretty place. The Appalachian Trail wove through the town. The town had many lakes. Your parents swam at Fayson Lakes all summer long. Our family joined a swim team there. The Fayson Lakes swim team belonged to the "A" Division. The "A" division teams had many strong swimmers. The swimmers, from ages six to eighteen, swam against other "A" team swimmers from nearby towns. Every Wednesday night and every Saturday morning a swim meet was held. Sometimes a special meet was held at Fayson on a Thursday night too. Whole families marched to the lake with picnics, swim snacks, blankets, towels, and team bathing suits to watch those meets. The mothers and fathers, like Dude and I, stood on the docks to help time the competition events. When we weren't on the docks we were cheering our heads off in the stands. "Go, Ryan! Go, Tanya!! Go, Rebecca!!!" Our children were good swimmers. Ryan and Rebecca liked the backstroke best. Tanya excelled at the breaststroke. One year she was the fastest breaststroke swimmer in her age group in our region, and we drove her all the way to West Point, New York, to participate in the Junior Olympics.

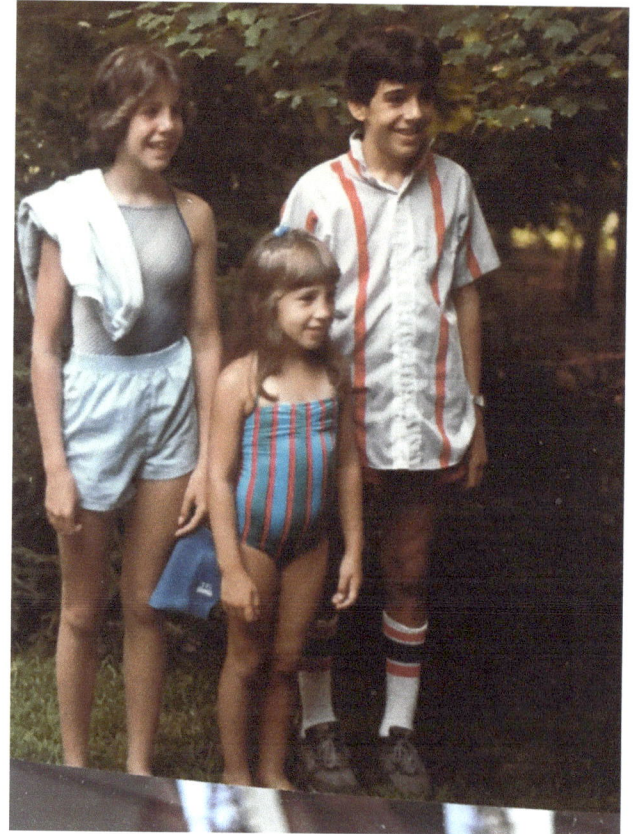

Here is a picture of the swim team in the year our little Rebecca joined. Can you find her and Tanya and Ryan? Our children got up early to go to swim practice. Practice for the older boys and girls started at 7 or 8 o'clock in the morning. Your parents often rode their bikes to swim practice at Fayson Lakes. Practice for the little kids didn't start until 9 o'clock. After practice we often hung out at the beach for the rest of the day when your parents were around the same ages that you are now.

Like all good parents, we tried to give our children many other experiences, besides swimming, when they were growing up. Ryan, Tanya, and Rebecca played T-ball and soccer and softball on our town's rec teams.

The girls took gymnastic lessons too.

As they grew older, the children learned to become good runners, and they participated in many cross-country meets.

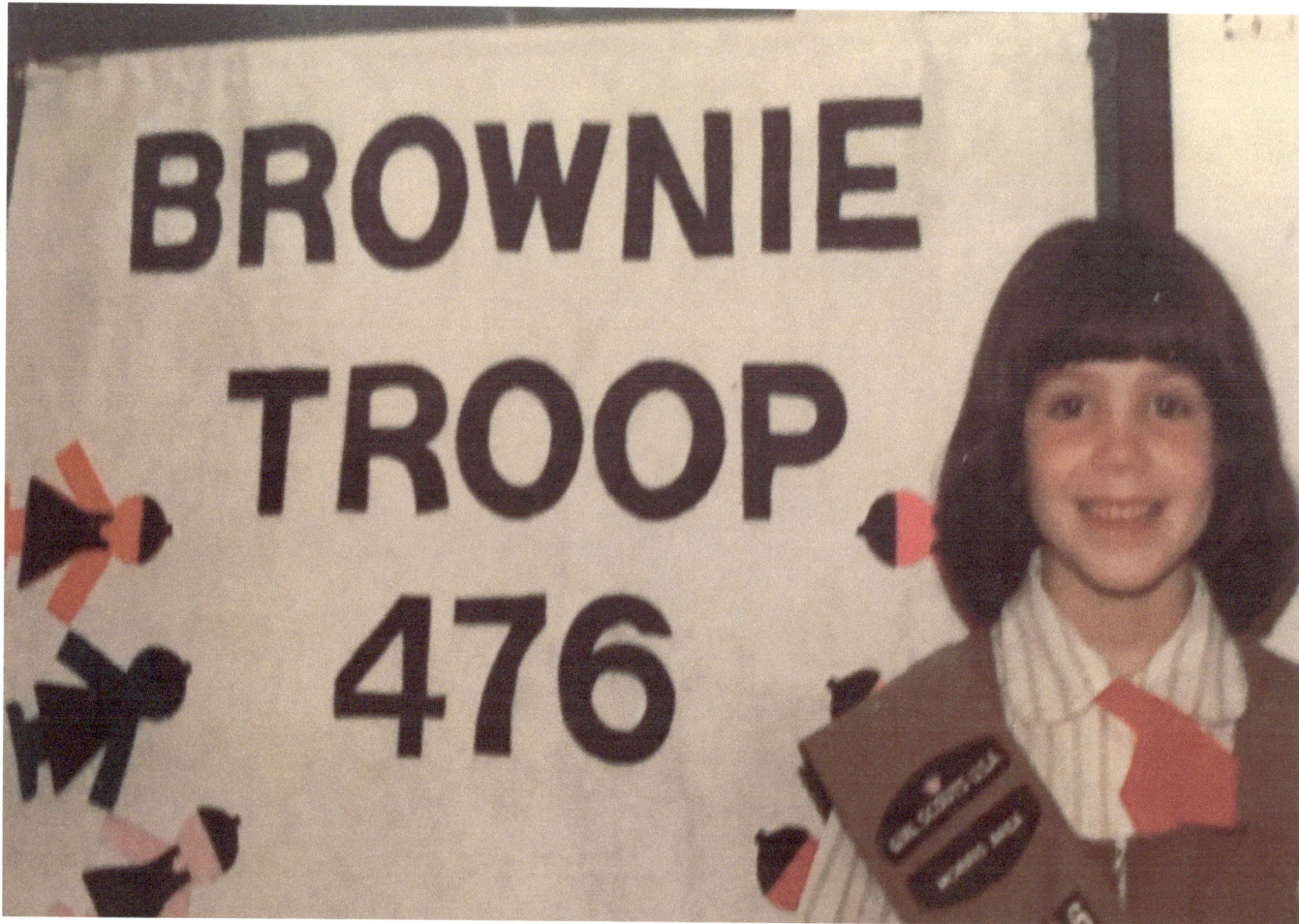

They belonged to Boy Scouts and Girl Scouts and Brownies.

Each year I made or bought the children a Halloween costume. I made this special clown costume and hat for Ryan when we lived for three years on Barrington Road in University Heights just outside Cleveland, Ohio. Over the years to follow, each of our children wore that clown costume on one Halloween.

Other special times for our family included birthday parties and Christmas. I loved planning birthday parties for our children. We had a red balloon party, a swimming party, a dress up costume party, a train ride party, a hiking party, a Billy Joel concert party, and a biking party at Lake Rickabear in Kinnelon, New Jersey, when our son Ryan was turning eleven. That was a scary party. Dude rode at the front of the line and nine little boys followed on their bikes. I rode at the end of the line on the dirt trails through the woods and around the lake. When we got to our meeting place at the end of the ride we only had eight boys. Yikes, we lost one! "Oh, no," Dude exclaimed. "What do we do?" I asked. We decided that I'd stay with the eight boys and Dude would ride off and try to find the missing boy whose name was Aaron. I was very worried. "What will I tell Aaron's mother?" I said to myself. Thankfully, about fifteen minutes later, Dude and Aaron emerged from the woods on their bikes. Aaron had decided to go off and explore a different trail. We were so relieved that we kept counting those boys again and again as we sat at a Rickabear picnic table and ate our birthday cupcakes.

When I was young my mother made me cupcakes for my birthdays too. She'd sometimes buy little toothpick flags and insert one on the top of each cupcake because I was born on Flag Day, June 14th.

Christmas was a very important holiday in our family. Each Christmas Eve we ate seven fish dishes. That was an Italian tradition. Some say that the seven-fish dinner represents the seven hills of Rome. Some say it represents the seven sacraments in the Catholic Church. But, wherever the tradition came from, we followed it. We made zeppola or salt cod cakes, haddock pie, and squid pie. We served salmon and sardines and shrimp and oysters and smoked bluefish or trout. The mothers of every generation worked for days to plan and prepare these dishes.

I loved Christmas because I love to give gifts to people. We always got a real Christmas tree, not an artificial one. A few times we cut the tree down in the woods near where we lived. I loved the sweet smell of balsam or fir that wafted through the house a day after we put up the tree. In 1968, the first year Dude and I had a tree, we made all the ornaments ourselves. We stuck a pin in a raw egg, drained it, washed it, painted pretty designs on the egg, then stuck a bit of wire in the hole to hang it on the tree. One of those eggs survives to this day.

Our children made handmade ornaments at school. As the years passed, the Christmas tree became more and more nostalgic. Usually those ornaments had the child's picture on them. Whenever we took a trip, I'd buy an ornament to remind us of that place. A Williamsburg drum. A Disney World Mickey Mouse. A Nantucket whale. A Ukranian egg from The Cathedral of St. John the Divine in New York City. A cranky nutcracker from the ballet we all saw together in 1986. A Native American memento from the Southwest where some of our oldest friends lived. A knitted Christmas tree, a gift from our children's crossing guard. Two limited edition Rockwell ornaments gifted by my mother. But the most important gifts from my mother were the beautifully crocheted ornaments, each one unique, that she made for me and our family members over the years. In 2010, the year that she died, I decorated the tree only with her white ornaments accented by little white lights. Here is a picture of my mother when she was eighty-eight years old. She was all dressed up for the wedding of Ryan and Amy in 2005. She lived to the age of ninety-three.

Dude and I loved raising our children. Those years were filled with many stories, many adventures, and many lost teeth.

Here is what Dude and I looked like during those years when we were raising our family. We were very busy and very tired and very happy.

Dude and I are proud that all three of our children were good students and graduated from college.

Ryan graduated from Tufts University in 1994.

Tanya graduated from Villanova University in 1996.

And Rebecca graduated from Yale University in the year 2000.

In the year 2001 Dude and I left New Jersey after living there for twenty-three years. We moved to Martha's Vineyard, a very beautiful place where we live now. We're so glad that you grandkids enjoy coming to hike and bike and swim with us during your summer vacations. Here is a picture of our house at 230 Pond Road in West Tisbury, Massachusetts. When we moved to the Martha's Vineyard house, there were no flowers around. Now we have flowers blooming during spring, summer, and fall. My dad loved to garden. I love to garden too. Our daughter Rebecca and her husband Chris got married in the back yard of this house in the year 2006.

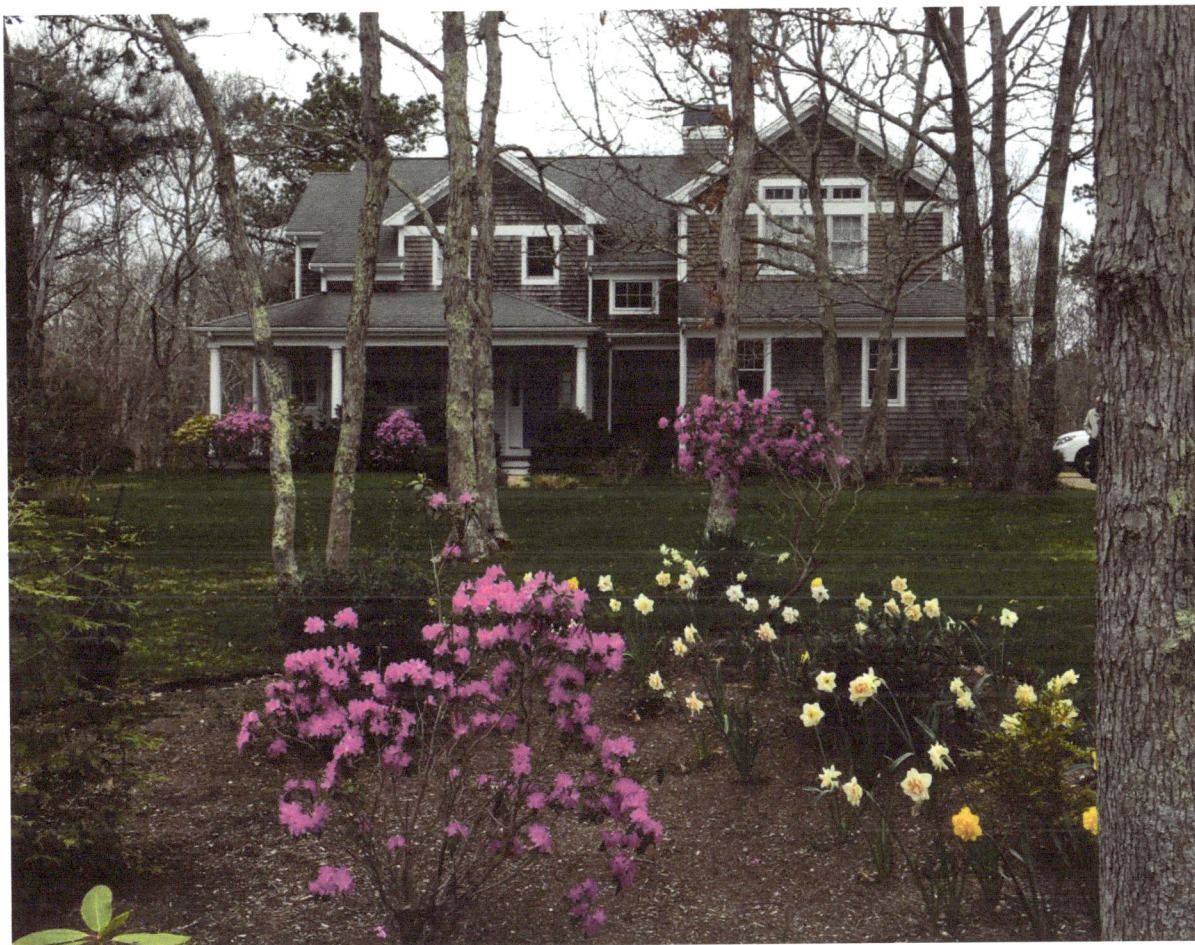

After they graduated from college and started their careers, each of our three children met someone they wanted to marry. Our family of five became a family of eight.

Then YOU, our beautiful grandchildren, came along.

Now we have thirteen people in our family: Dude and I and all the people in this picture.

As you grow older you will learn how fast the years fly by. One day you may be telling your grandchildren your stories, just as I have told mine today.

THINGS TO THINK ABOUT

1. Can you describe some ways that life has changed since your ancestors lived?

2. Is there anyone in these stories who you would have liked to meet in person?

3. Some of your ancestors were very brave. They learned how to overcome adversity. Adversity happens when life gets very sad or difficult. Which stories show people who overcame adversity?

4. Do you think you are like any of the people in these stories?

5. Ask your parents to tell you more stories about some of the other relatives in your family tree.

www.ingramcontent.com/pod-product-compliance
Lightning Source LLC
Chambersburg PA
CBHW040452100426

42813CB00021BA/2978